AF338142

CAN I DANCE ON THE MOON?
ALL ABOUT GRAVITY

Physics Book Grade 6
Children's Physics Books

What would it be like to stand on the Moon and try to dance? Would you just float away? Let's find out how gravity works, on Earth, on our Moon, and everywhere.

WHAT IS GRAVITY?

Gravity is one of the basic forces in the universe. It tries to pull together any objects that have mass. The more mass an object has, the more its gravity pulls on every other object with mass.

Any physical object has mass. That means an apple has mass but an idea of an apple in your head does not have mass.

And here's a funny thing: we know a lot about gravity and what it does, but we don't yet know why it does it. Nobody knows what causes gravity!

Quark
Star

THE PULL OF GRAVITY

We live on the Earth. Our bodies have mass and the Earth has mass, and your gravity pulls on the Earth as it uses its gravity to pull you closer to it. The difference, of course, is that the Earth has so much more mass than you do that your gravitational field doesn't have much effect on the Earth.

However, the Earth's gravity is what keeps you, the stones on the ground, the water in the ocean and the air in the sky from floating off into space!

Earth's gravity pulls you down toward the center of the planet at a constant rate, every second of every day. Try jumping: your upward force overcomes gravity for a little bit and lifts you into the air, but pretty soon gravity's pull overcomes your upward force and pulls you back down again.

Most of the day we don't notice the pull of gravity. We were born on the Earth and we are used to dealing with its gravity from the moment we start to crawl. But you realize the power of gravity if you slip and lose your footing: almost before you know what is going on, gravity has slammed you down to the ground!

DISTANCE MATTERS

Although the pull of gravity gets less and less the further you are from an object, it never gets to zero. So every star you see twinkling in the night sky is exerting its gravitational pull on you, but from so far away that that pull can barely be detected.

The planet Jupiter has much more mass than the Moon does, but it is so far away from us that its gravitational pull is tiny. The Moon, on the other hand, is close enough to the Earth and has enough mass that its gravitational pull affects us. The Moon's gravity makes the tides in Earth's oceans! The Baby Professor book Ocean Tides and Tsunamis can tell you more about this.

FALLING OBJECTS

n 1589, Italian scientist Galileo Galilei wanted to know what would happen if you drop two balls, one much heavier than the other, from the same height at the same time. Would the heavier ball hit the ground first?

GALILEO GALILEI

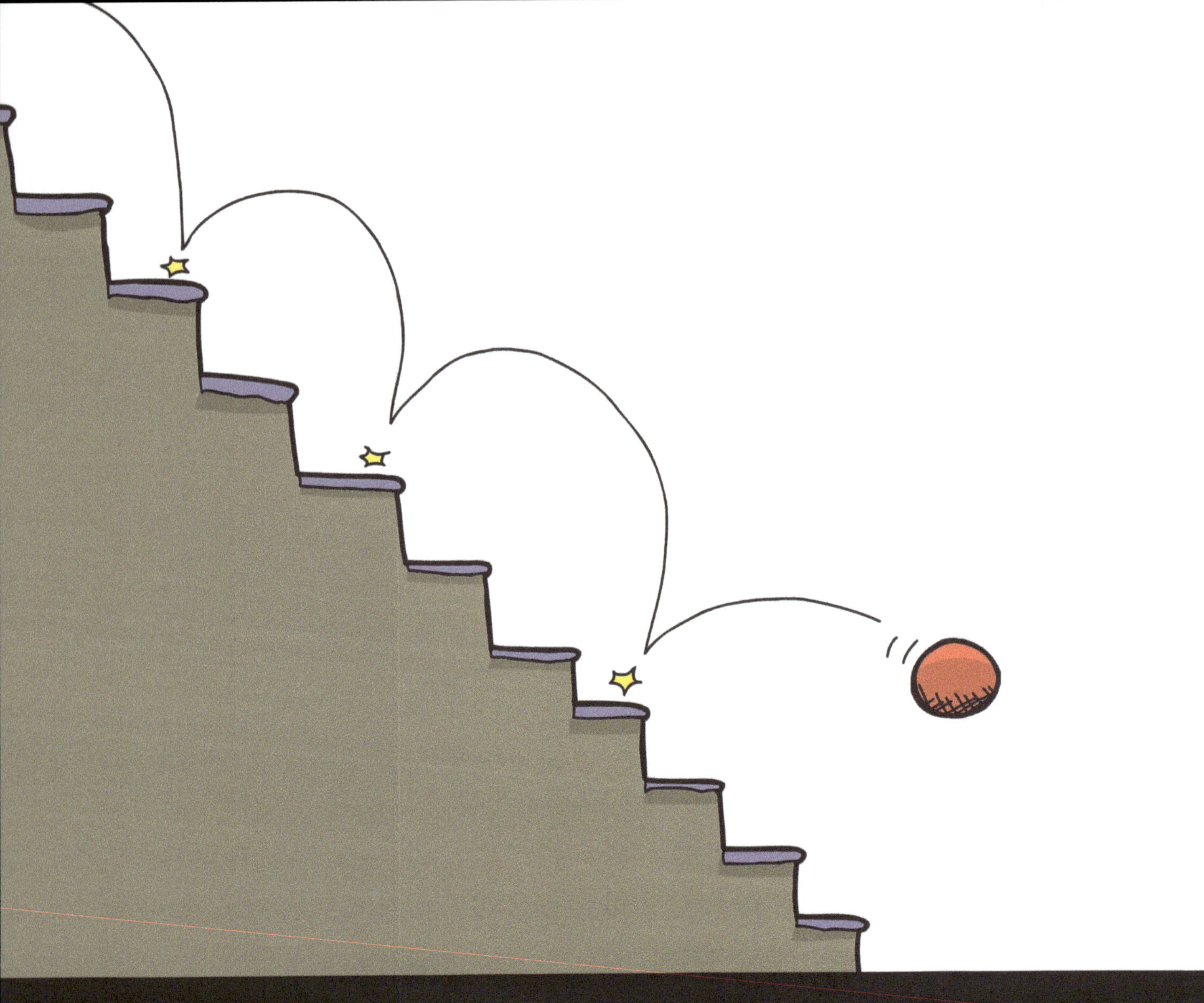

He found out, by actually dropping two balls from a tower, that the balls hit the ground at the same time!

Although the mass of the balls was different, the pull of gravity on them was the same.

Gravity works the same on all objects with mass. The only way to fight gravity would be with another force: for instance, if Galileo had tied a parachute to one of the balls, air resistance would have slowed that ball's fall and it would have hit the ground later than the other ball.

MASS, GRAVITY, AND WEIGHT

Mass is not weight. Mass is the atoms an object is made of, and how tightly together they are packed. Imagine a bowling ball and a balloon that is the same size. The bowling ball has much more mass than the balloon, because its atoms are denser and more closely packed together than the air molecules that are inside the balloon.

BOWLING BALL

Your mass is the same, whether you are on the Earth or in outer space or standing on the Moon. But your weight would be different, depending on where you are. Your weight is the result of gravity working on your mass.

Let's pretend you weigh 150 pounds on Earth. That's Earth's gravity working on your mass. Let's see what you would weigh if you visited other places in our solar system.

Jupiter is much more massive than the Earth, so if you could stand on Jupiter (a problem because its surface is mostly gas!), you would weigh over 350 pounds.

A HOVER ON MARS

If you visited Mars, whose gravity is less than Earth's, you would weigh 57 pounds. If you landed on our Moon, which has even less mass and where gravity is even less, you would weigh just under 25 pounds.

And if you visited Pluto, the dwarf planet at the edge of our solar system, you would weigh less than ten pounds because its gravity is so much smaller than Earth's.

Your weight equals your mass times the surface gravity of the planet you are standing on.

DANCING ON THE MOON?

We started by wondering what would happen if you tried to dance on the Moon. Since the Moon has mass, you would not just float away from its surface.

But the gravity of the Moon is only about 16 percent of the gravity we are used to here on Earth. And that means a lot of fast dance moves would not work very well at all on the Moon: every time you stamped your foot down, you would bounce into the air!

So, yes: you can dance on the Moon: but you'll do better if you choose a slow dance rather than a fast, bouncy one…and you can forget about hip hop altogether!

THE MOON

HIGH JUMPING

What you might be interested in, instead of dancing, is a jumping contest. Of course, the effect of gravity would be the same on everybody in the contest if you are all on the Moon, so you would all get the same advantage.

But let's say that, in our contest, each player is on a different planet. We want to see how high they can jump.

On Earth, Player One jumps a foot and a half in the air. Not bad!

PLANET JUPITER

On Jupiter, where the force of gravity is three hundred times greater than on Earth, Player Two can hardly jump at all. Thanks for playing!

Player Three, on Mars, makes a beautiful jump six feet off the ground.

Player Four, on our Moon, takes the lead with a jump more than twelve feet off the surface!

But sneaky Player Five chose to jump on Enceladus, a tiny moon orbiting Saturn. Enceladus is only 14 percent the diameter of the Earth, and its gravitation pull is so small that Player Five rises 140 feet off the moon's surface before floating back down. Prize to Player Five!

ENCELADUS

Tides Caused by Gravitational Force of the Moon

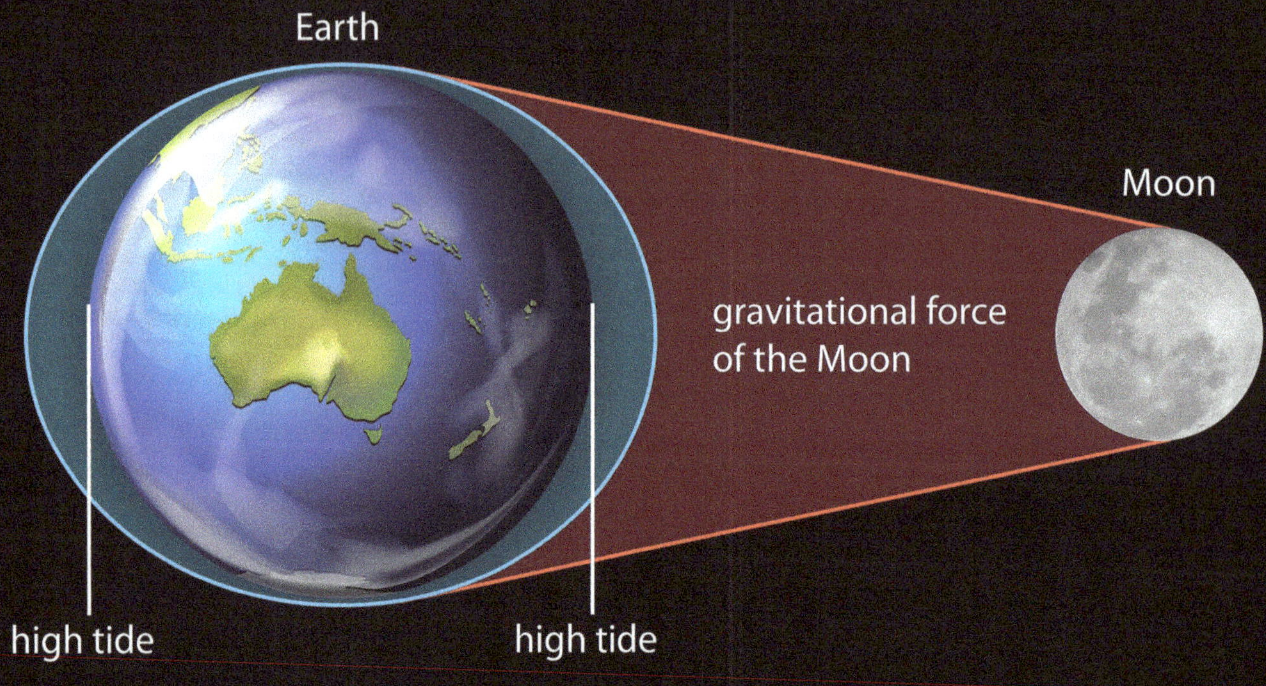

GRAVITY AND ORBITS

If the Earth's gravity is always pulling things down toward the center of the Earth, how can satellites stay in orbit? It's because a second force is involved.

The force of gravity is a centripetal force. That is from a Latin word meaning "to the center".

The second force is in play because the satellites are not just falling toward the Earth. They are moving so fast that, if there were no gravity, they would shoot away from the Earth into space. Their speed generates a centrifugal force pushing the satellites outward. "Centrifugal" is from the Latin word for "running away from the center."

A SATELLITE

When we launch satellites, we try to put them where the centrifugal force generated by their speed matches the centripetal force the Earth's gravity causes. When we get that right, the satellite, or the International Space Station, is in a stable orbit around the Earth and can keep on zooming around and around the planet.

MICROGRAVITY

Microgravity is sometimes called "free fall". You can experience this on a roller coaster ride at an amusement park. The roller coaster car, which has much more mass than you do, carries you up and up to the top of the highest curve on the track.

MICROGRAVITY ON A ROLLERCOASTER RIDE

Then, as you go over the top and start down the other side, for a short while you and the car are falling at the same speed toward the Earth, faster than the speed gravity gives you. For a moment you seem to float in the air, because you and the car are in a microgravity different from the Earth's gravity.

SUPERGRAVITY

Maybe the strangest objects in the universe are black holes, objects so massive that nothing can escape their gravity, not even light (which is why they are, um, black)! The gravity in a black hole pulls everything toward its center and lets nothing escape.

BLACK HOLE

Black holes can even swallow planets and stars, and there may be millions of black holes in our galaxy, the Milky Way. Fortunately, we haven't found any black holes anywhere near our solar system…yet!

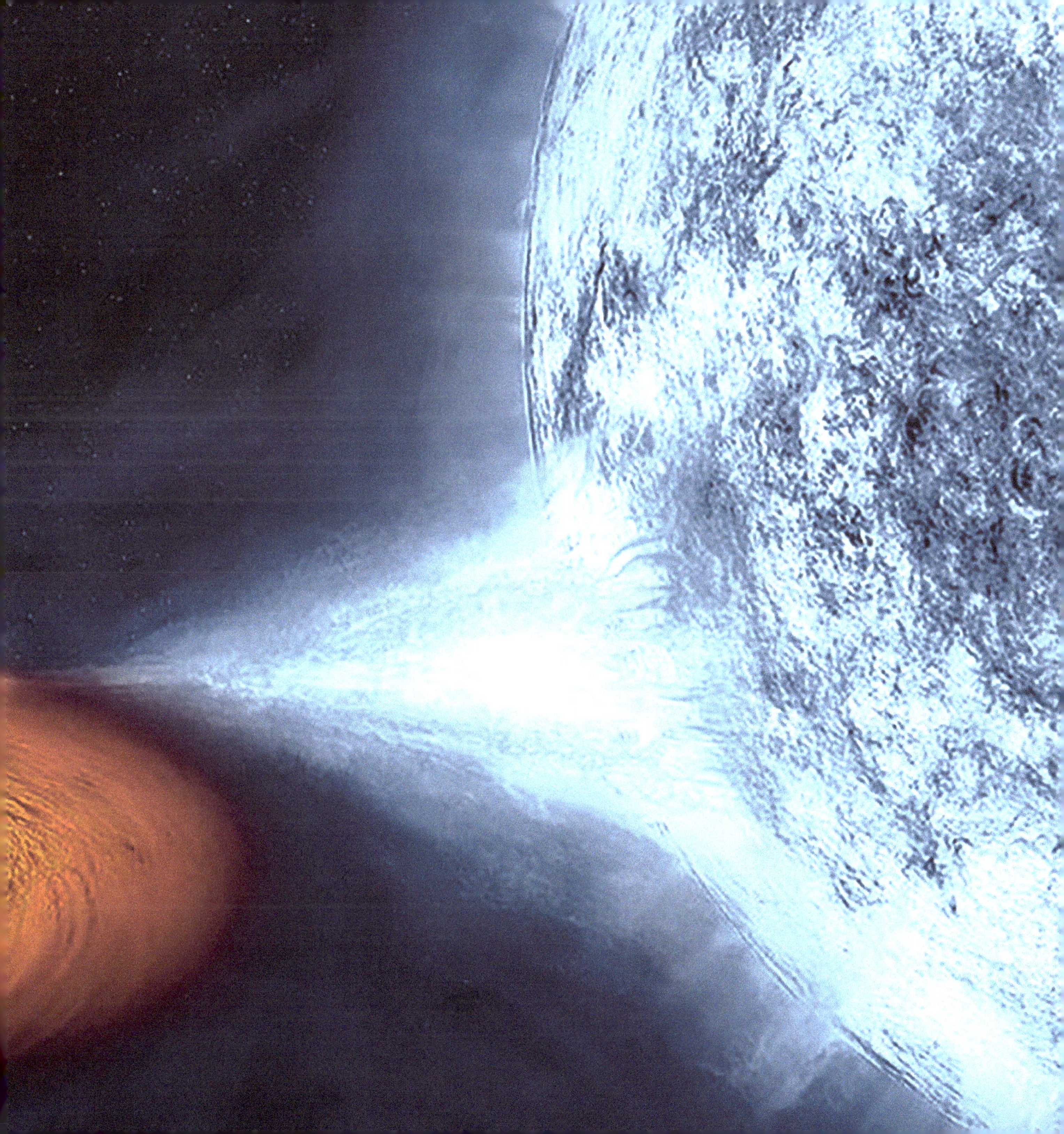

SPACE EXPLORER!

Even just standing here on Earth, you can learn a lot about the Moon, the other planets, and the universe beyond. Read Baby Professor books like A Space Ride to Saturn! to learn more about our planet and our whole universe.

Visit
BABY PROFESSOR
EDUCATION KIDS
www.BabyProfessorBooks.com
to download Free Baby Professor eBooks
and view our catalog of new and exciting
Children's Books

www.ingramcontent.com/pod-product-compliance
Lightning Source LLC
Chambersburg PA
CBHW041935110726
48010CB00003B/115